VICTORIAN
INTERIORS

ROOM

BY

ROOM

GLOUCESTER MASSACHUSETTS

ROCKPORT PUBLISHERS

KATHRYN LIVINGSTON

First published in the United States of America by
Rockport Publishers, Inc.
33 Commercial Street
Gloucester, Massachusetts 01930-5089
Telephone: (978) 282-9590
Facsimile: (978) 283-2742

Distributed to the book trade and art trade in the United States by
North Light Books, an imprint of
F & W Publications
1507 Dana Avenue
Cincinnati, Ohio 45207
Telephone: (800) 289-0963

Other distribution by
Rockport Publishers, Inc.
Gloucester, Massachusetts 01930-5089

ISBN 1-56496-424-8

10 9 8 7 6 5 4 3 2 1

Design: Argus Visual Communication, Boston
Layout: SYP Design & Production
Cover Image: Design: Miriam Wohlberg;
Photo: Bill Rothschild

Printed in China

Dedication

To Russell, whose instinct for scale and understanding of English furniture taught me to see a room with fresh eyes.

Acknowledgments

Various people have been extremely helpful during the preparation of this book. First, I would like to express my heartfelt appreciation to the entire staff at Rockport Publishers. I owe particular thanks to Rosalie Grattaroti, Acquisitions Editor, who conceived the *Room by Room* series of books and invited me to select the illustrations and write the text for *Victorian Interiors*. Her propulsive energy, upbeat outlook on life and endless publishing wisdom made working with her a thorough delight. A great deal of my gratitude goes to Martha Wetherill, now also in Acquisitions, for her fine-tuned editorial instinct and eye. Her vision has accompanied all four volumes through every stage of production, to provide a series that is beautiful to look at as well as enjoyable. I would like to express my great indebtedness to the book's editor Jeanine Caunt, who gave me always excellent advice. Her editorial know-how, kind encouragement and grace under pressure were a constant source of strength and inspiration to me. I am very grateful to David Cottingham, whose skillful and sensitive copyediting made all the difference in the text. Finally, of paramount importance to a visual book of this nature is its own graphic format. Without the impact of the highly creative design of Sara Day, it would have been hard to convey all the romance, adventure and practical relevance *Victorian Interiors* can bring to contemporary decor.

At the heart and soul of this book lies the innovative urge and educated sensibility of the tastemaking decorators and photographers whose works are featured on its pages. These talented people walk us through a series of remarkable spaces that open up, room by room, all kinds of new reasons for the revival of interest in Victorian furnishings, color schemes and richly detailed decorative elements. It is through their various clever interpretations of what is Victorian that we learn many worthy ways certain pieces or certain design notions can be easily integrated into today's romantic, traditional or even contemporary home environment.

Finally, my deep-felt thanks go to two very special and gifted people, Carol Meredith and Bill Rothschild, who have both been major contributors to several past Rockport publications. Without their generous help in both the textual and photographic areas of *Room by Room: Victorian Interiors* this book would not have been possible.

Contents

Mary Knackstedt *Foreword*

The Victorian era (1837 to 1901) was a romantic and, in many respects, a very sensual period. But it was also eclectic, allowing for wide-ranging personal tastes and styles. It went to extremes of femininity and masculinity—because it was a time of extremes—the birth of the Machine Age, and a period during which handcrafted decorative arts were prized. Through a tremendous variety of fascinating interiors, this book illustrates this Victorian tendency toward extremes, exaggerations, and eclecticism.

The Victorian period was a time when a man's home was considered his castle, and the center of family life. As a result, architecture began to emerge as a profession. The coming of the railroad made traveling easier, and merchants could provide goods such as Turkish carpets, paisley printed fabrics, and hand-printed wallcoverings. The U.S. was still strongly influenced by all things British. There was a hunger for fine things, a nostalgia for extravagant times past, and a romantic sentimentality which characterized much of the design of the era. If the desired items weren't available here, the wealthy would bring craftsmen and their families over from Europe. For those who weren't wealthy, there were do-it-yourself publications, so they could learn to create objects that are now antiques. People respected the crafts and saw their furnishings as treasures. Many of today's Victorian treasures survived because they have special meaning for their owners, or because the pieces themselves possess unique personality.

If you have seen Victorian items that you didn't care for, investigate a little further with this book. There is something for every taste. We can learn about the styles, traditions, arts and crafts of this era in many ways, and through personal experience at the National Victorian Society at the Athenaeum in Philadelphia. Today, we are so busy that it may be hard to imagine a time when the wealthy and the upper middle classes had considerable time to enjoy the arts and amenities of life. Most fine houses had parlors or music rooms. Although the Victorians didn't have indoor plumbing or electricity, a lot of daily life was similar to our own. The shapes of the rooms are not that different from ours.

As a designer, I deal with human factors, or *proxemics*. Many physical, cultural, and social issues are illustrated by the architecture of the Victorian era. The high ceilings and numerous windows helped maintain comfortable temperatures in the heat of summer. This is why railway stations of this period have high ceilings. Both personal and public spaces have interesting scale and embellishments. The Victorian era has more than just beautiful artifacts. This era can teach us a lot that is practical, human, and comfortable.

The dining room of the Victorian Merchant's House in Harrisburg, Pennsylvania, reflects the East-meets-West eclecticism favored by America's achieving classes of the 1800s. The house was built in 1867 by William Bell of Pittsburgh, then sold to a merchant named Barringer. Its structure is unusual in that it runs the full length of the property. It was never cut up in any way, and the original woodwork and other characteristics remain intact. Design: Mary Knackstedt; Photo: Bill Rothschild

Introduction

Kathryn Livingston

The word *Victorian* conjures up all kinds of visual extravagances: masses of white embroidered curtains billowing about a romantic four-poster bed frothed with antique linens and lace; the glowing opulence of delicately curved brass and etched-glass lamps paving the way for a sensational wooden staircase traced with highly patterned wallpaper and Oriental carpets; a plump, deeply button-upholstered sofa with a sinuous frame so ornately carved it looks more like sculpture than furniture.

Our renewed interest in the magical whimsies, fanciful filigrees, and exuberant details of Victorian styles may be a desire to trade reality for the mystery of dreams. Victorian times, like ours, were full of scientific innovations, rapid change, and social turbulence. Not unlike the Victorians, sometimes overwhelmed by contemporary pace, we tend to view the home as a soft, warm, private sanctuary and idyllic personalized escape place.

Though we think of the Victorian Age as one of ostentatious propriety and stifling piety, aesthetically it was adventurous. It was terrifically daring in its mixture of motifs and materials, eclectic and exotic in its cultural sources. These included the Japanese and Chinese, Stuart and Tudor England, Indian and American Indian, Islamic and Greco-Egyptian, the Italian Renaissance and eighteenth-century France.

The era also spawned its own distinct styles. One of these is American Gothic, best exemplified by the exteriors and interiors of wooden-gingerbread prairie farmhouses and manorial brick strongholds across the United States and Canada, where the useful artifacts of pioneering and the aspirations of newly wealthy mineral kings and railroad builders, who liked to imitate British landed gentry, melded into unique design expressions. Another was the Aesthetic Reform Movement led in England by William Morris, with his meticulously handcrafted furniture such as the famous Morris chair, and spearheaded in America by Louis Comfort Tiffany with his leaded favrile glass lamps and semi-abstract, nature-inspired stained-glass windows. Art Nouveau, which originated on the continent and takes its name from a shop that opened in Paris in 1895, flowered in Victorian England and America and, as it developed, twined with Gothic, Celtic, and pre-Raphaelite imagery and the Victorian obsession with bringing outdoors indoors through such nature-inspired fantasy motifs as swirling trees, voluptuous clouds, and undulating nymphs. Finally, a reaction against the factory-produced furniture and curlicued excesses of some of the more vulgar Victorian showiness manifested itself in the Arts and Crafts Movement—first in England and then in America. With its muscular, angular, sometimes austere furnishings showing hammerblows and pegged timbers, it is generally thought to be the first move forward to fuss-free modern design.

Of course, at the center of the Victorian age is the eighteen-year-old, only-child princess who became Queen of the United Kingdom of Great Britain and Ireland and Empress of India. Though Queen Victoria was born in Kensington Palace on May 24, 1819, the Victorian era begins with her accession to the throne in 1837, and ends with her death in the first month of the new century, in January 1901.

Victoria's long reign—the longest of any monarch's in British history—was a period of unprecedented material prosperity. During this time, on the strength of the Industrial Revolution and a vigorous imperial policy, England became the political and cultural leader of the world. The queen was accepted as the worthiest symbol of a great nation and an unparalleled empire. Significant historical events took place during these decades: for England, Roberts in South Africa, Kitchener at Khartoum, and the acquisition of Suez; on the Continent, Garibaldi's unification of Italy and Bismarck's unification of Germany. For the United States, the Victorian Age coincided with the settling of the West, the Civil War, the building of great industrial empires—and with them an important epoch in American taste, so well described by Edith Wharton in *The Age of Innocence.*

India was always particularly near Queen Victoria's heart. She encouraged her viceroys to write her long, detailed, personal letters. The mingling of British and Indian lifestyles during the Raj had enormous impact on the creative sparks of London architects and designers. As influential British Victorians became enamored with the many exotic colors, patterns, fabrics, and shapes of Victoria's colonies, their broadened horizons were followed by the world. Meanwhile, machines empowered the burgeoning middle class. Freed from drudgery, they wholeheartedly embraced the abundance of new products—many newly mass-produced, others surfacing from the far-flung corners of the earth. The middle classes liked a royal household that combined the advantages of royalty and virtue and in which they seemed to see the ideal image of the very lives they led themselves. Duty, industry, morality, and domesticity had triumphed; and the very chairs and tables Victoria, Albert, and their children favored became symbols. These objects met with singular responsiveness and assumed the forms of prim solidity. The Victorian age was in full swing when the Great Exhibition of 1851 opened in the Crystal Palace in Hyde Park, giving material expression to the new ideals and forces. Among the exhibits were model English cottages and new techniques of furniture construction, as well as rickshaws and Chinese wallpapers, Moorish textiles, and black-lacquered papier-mâché chairs with pearly inlays. It all stimulated an almost wild mixing of period inspiration and eclectic excitement.

The Victorian era is generally divided into three design periods, Early, Middle, and Late, with the Middle taking all the blame for the exaggerated, clunky, over-the-top elements. Today, many of these soaring beds and colossal Gothic sideboards seem almost humorous. Since wit is an important design ingredient now, these once-shunned pieces—standing alone in a minimalist modern loft—can make riveting statements. So can the endearingly named Victorian oddities with nearly equally eccentric forms: whatnots and gypsy tables, Berlin-beaded puffs and one-armed Chesterfields, Turkish rockers with sprung seats, and japanned breakfronts with myriad arches and pinnacles.

As we head toward the next century, one thing is patently clear: our yearning for the charming wallpapers, unabashedly romantic furnishings, the refreshing blendings of outdoors and indoors—in fact, all the sentimental appreciation of the past that the Victorians introduced us to—is more meaningful than ever.

Victorian Entrances

Victorians placed a high premium on first impressions and their lasting effects. Because of these sentiments, much of the prettiness and plenitude of Victoriana was enlisted in decorating the entryway to create a proper greeting.

The nineteenth-century hallway played a much more important role in transmitting the tone and tenor of the rest of the home than it does today. Victorians believed that the moment you opened the front door, you had to convey a feeling of inviting warmth and felicitous respectability. Their entryway was less of a transient connector, leading people from one place to another, than an actual room with an eminent value and distinct function. It was the site of certain ritualistic social preliminaries. Here, bon mots were exchanged while coats were unbuttoned, capes were slipped off, and complicated hair styles were checked after hats came off. Eager to put her best foot forward, the hostess right away extended herself, graciously offering the visitor a warming cup of tea or a glass of sherry, especially if a considerable journey had preceded the arrival. To accommodate all these niceties, the hallway was often furnished as if it were a miniature sitting room or auxiliary living room. A small table and a pair of wicker chairs or a shapely upholstered settee helped embellish the exuberance of the welcome and provided immediate seating for light conversation.

Many of the hallmarks of the Victorian entrance fit beautifully into a contemporary design scheme with a romantic bent or a flair for drama. Perhaps foremost of these is an ornately carved wooden staircase, quickly followed by the all-important halltree. Bristling with pegs, it stands at attention close to the door, a highly decorative device for hanging coats and hats. An amply detailed, wood-framed mirror with a slightly altar-like outline—essential so that Victorians could check their appearances before making a grand entrance during parties—can add both an illusion of spaciousness as well as a certain dignity and occasion to the entryway. Functioning similarly is another frequent feature of Victorian hallways borrowed from ecclesiastic architecture: stained glass. It creates an artful diffusion of light and adds a Renaissance richness. A marble shelf—often part of the hall tree or the mirror—is an ideal receptacle for keys, mail, or loose change.

Victorians loved Oriental rugs, fancy ceilings, splashy wallpapers, and fresh greenery at least as much as we do today. Exquisitely bordered runners on stairs, finely defined moldings, and gay jardinières enlivened then, as they can now, even the most formal gateway into a home watched by a stern but benevolent grandfather clock.

A spectacular stained-glass window and a richly carved stairway, celebrated by a solemn runner, statuesque lamp, and grandiose clock, express the Victorian idea that there is a built-in morality connected simply with the presence of Gothic furnishings in the house. Design: Richard and Patricia Kent with Ron Kanani Photo: Dave Marlow/Aspen

The deep-tinctured luxuriance of wallpaper, wood, and rug lighten up with the unabashed romance radiating from the painting, the profusion of fresh flowers, and the playful gilt ebony Regency jardinière, which echoes the more irreverent era that just preceded the Victorians. Design: Marilyn Katz; Photo: Bill Rothschild

Reaching celestial heights of the opulent art of Victorian welcome, this entrance hall to a Colorado silver king's domain is graced by an ornate wooden stairway, heady brass-and-glass light fixtures, starry walls and fancy coffered ceilings. It also serves as an auxiliary living room. Design: Richard and Patricia Kent with Ron Kanan; Photo: Dave Marlow/Aspen

Magnificent woodwork—with its masterful detailing and eclectic late-Victorian experimentation with Greek and Oriental motifs as well as the beginings of the Arts and Crafts Movement—gains further momentum from an 1890s-style wallpaper bursting with cabbage roses. Design: Marcy Balk; Photo: Peter Peirce

Elevated luminosity—set off by sixteen etched-glass balloon shades, shining brass, and icy crystal—manifests the Victorian obsession with wondrous ceilings, pretty moldings, and surprising windows. It is the double-chandeliered entrance hall of China Cabin, the historic boat off Tiburon, California. Design: *Historic Preservation* magazine; Photo: David Duncan Livingston

Linen-white paint freshens up a venerable Victorian stairwell's delightful decorative detailing of bead-and-panel woodworks, as does the charming rose-and-maize palette of the wallpaper, antique quilt, and cable-crocheted banister throw. Design: Lois Weir; Photo: Tony Giammarino

Folksy American Victoriana at its sophisticated best revolves around a
marvelously whimsical nineteenth-century hall tree and an authentic
period pinewood rocker covered with a patchwork quilt in this delightfully
busy, lived-in entrance full of colorful handcrafted bric-a-brac. Design:
Tonin MacCallun; Photo: © image/dennis krukowski

Lighthearted flower-strewn wallpaper—something the Victorians introduced us to—covers this small entryway with blue and all the charms of the past. It creates a welcoming backdrop for three entrance essentials, each of which is a very special and romantic antique piece: a nineteenth-century giltwood mirror, a shapely glass lamp tinkling with crystal drops, and a delicate little hall table with an edged marble top. Design: Tonin MacCallum; Photo: © image/dennis krukowski

Carpeting reminiscent of Victorian wallpapers enlivens the exquisite staircase and cozy entry space created by the balustrade's twists and turns. A marble-topped console, a giltwood mirror, and architectural drawings and maquettes—beloved by Victorians—invite interest in the rest of the house. Design: Mark Hampton; Photo: Stan Rumbough

The sense of containment and formality of this foyer issue from its luminous original Victorian ceiling. Indirect lighting from above, the dark intensity of teal-blue paneling, and the diamond precision of stenciled floors all take their cues from its coffered beauty. Design: Anthony Catalfano; Photo: Steve Vierra

Ribbons and roses and other Victorian design elements such as the needlepoint rug and an indulgence in delightful chintz fabrics provide the kind of romance we often crave today. A splendidly decorative settee welcomes near the hallway stairs—as it did in the nineteenth century. Design: Dianne Chapman; Photo: David Duncan Livingston

The Victorian American West comes full blast in the
doorway of this Rocky Mountain ranch, with its
authentic beveled glass, metal bars and artful hinges,
old beaded paneling, an evocative watercolor depicting high-plains braves, and a rusty old saddle peg
cobbled together from horseshoes. Design: Zoe
Compton; Photo: Dave Marlow/Aspen

Chaps, spurs, lassos, ornate leather saddles, as well
as down vests and water-repellent jackets decorate
the wonderful Western Victorian wall of old and new
panels, log-cabin wainscoting, slat floors, and twig
ceilings in the mud room part of the entrance, which
leads to both downstairs stables and upstairs living
quarters. Design: Zoe Compton; Photo: Dave
Marlow/Aspen

The Old West, New West, and Victoriana
meet in the upstairs hallway, where nineteenth-century woodwork quietly frames
an extraordinary collection of frontier-fla-
vored paraphernalia, including a leather-
belted mirror, Native American figurines,
a wooden guest book, and bronze buffalo
merry-go-round chandelier. Design: Zoe
Compton; Photo: Dave Marlow/Aspen

A typical Victorian hall tree with its neo-Gothic wood-framed mirror and
alabaster shelf for keys and cigars protrudes its many pegs for hats and
extends its gently curved arms to receive walking sticks and umbrellas.
Paisley wallpaper, tattersall blankets, and hunt-country accessories
shift this entrance to some decidedly masculine aspects of Victorian
design. Design: Marjorie Matthews; Photo: Bill Rothschild

Chucking out the frills and swirls, this Western entry nevertheless retains much of the Victorian ways of greeting. Though done with rough-hewn woods and handloomed Navajo weaves, here are all the Victorian hallway standards: amusing hall tree, impressive stairway, comforting seat. Design: Marjorie Shushan; Photo: Dave Marlow/Aspen

Late Victorians leaning towards the American Arts and Crafts movement forever sought to bring nature indoors with fresh air, sleeping porches, and motifs reflecting regional flora and fauna. This former sleeping porch, with its wild-duck pillows and woodsy furnishings, now serves as both entrance way and secondary family room. Design: Martin Kuckly, Kuckly Associates, Inc.; Photo: Bill Rothschild

American Victorian gingerbread at its most enchanting arches its trellised charms around a lovely San Francisco house and frames pretty cameo views of the rest of the period neighborhood. A decorative entrance like this wears nothing but gray deck paint on its floor and a regularly refreshed snowy coating on its superb fretwork. Design: *Historic Preservation* magazine; Photo: David Duncan Livingston

As American as apple pie and the Fourth of July, a cozy corner of a hundred foot-long, hundred year-old Long Island entry porch is cooled by ancient oaks and hickory trees. With its white wicker rockers and armchairs, it invites good talk and socializing over cups of fragrant tea on languid summer afternoons. Design: Lois Weir; Photo: Tony Giammarino

The dreamy essence of homespun American perfection, this verandah entrance to a seaside family retreat is design that works with, instead of against, nature. All the beauty of a summer day comes streaming through the beguiling gingerbread and airy white wicker with a technicolor burst of hanging flower baskets and a patriotic pillow, as in Victorian times, hand-stitched by loving hands. Design: Shane Miller; Photo: Tony Giammarino

As in an English cottage of Victorian times, this entrance from the garden ushers in its own gust of flowering greenery and summertime cheer. Blue wicker chairs, botanical prints, frilly eyelet curtains bouncing off twiney twigs, and a needlepoint hanging abloom with roses create a gazebo feeling. Design: Eugenie Kim; Photo: Bill Rothschild

A set of white-painted, bentwood Adirondack rockers is all the frosting this wonderful old gingerbreaded front porch needs. Its glass-enclosed comforts make a great people-watching hideaway as well as an intriguing entry point into a house encrusted with history. Design: *Historic Preservation* magazine; Photo: David Duncan Livingston

The enthrallingly airy sweep and soar of frosty-white wooden porchposts and delicately carved lacework of spandrels and gingerbread brackets wrap the circumference of this breathtaking Virginia country mansion and create the kind of dreamy romantic entrance that stakes a permanent claim on a visitor's memory. Design: Jenny and Bob Salzmann; Photo: Tony Giammarino

A brilliant-hued spiral of cast iron—a metal very much favored in the late-Victorian era for both building fixtures and garden furnishings—becomes the decorative connector of a two-storied, part-indoor, part-outdoor entryway to a romantic, wicker-filled townhouse. Photo: Courtesy of The Iron Shop

An entrance from the sea makes a bracing approach to the good life. This white-columned blue haven melds many Victorian fancies with a shot of contemporary sensuality, sportiness, and wit. Take the painted finish tropical fish motif of the watermelon server which coasts on four metal turtle feet. Think of the barefoot life appeal of the splendid handpainted floor and the carefree abandon of the crisp stripe-upholstered white wicker chairs. Design: Roger Bartels; Photo: Tony Giammarino

Arabic form and ornament left a deep impression on London's Victorian architects, who traveled extensively in the Middle East during the 1850s. This elegantly exotic entrance to a historic mansion sports an Islamic-style wallpaper, zebra-and-tiger prints, alabaster seating, and a quirky birdcage from Victoria's tropical colonies. Design: Miriam Wohlberg; Photo: Bill Rothschild

This same Orientalist-papered, spacious entrance hall features lavishly draped seating of silks and velvets. With its fancy *recamier* curled up at the foot and cushioned with typical Victorian needlework—such as the Berlin-beaded bird motif—the corner functions very much in nineteenth-century fashion, as an auxiliary sitting room. Design: Miriam Wohlberg; Photo: Bill Rothschild

Stately reassurance meets you at the door of this tradtional entrance based on Victorian tenets that will never go out of style. To name a few: welcoming Oriental rugs, a pretty settee beside a fine staircase stenciled to match the walls; the richness of carved dark wood against ferns and flowers, brass and gold. Design: Dennis Pendalari; Photo: Steve Vierra

A shapely Victorian mirror-fronted, bleached-pine armoire sets the tone of nostalgia for the Old West in this New West entrance. With local cactus and an open, beamed living room, everything new in the space suggests bygone objects. Design: Peggy Rogers; Photo: Dave Marlow/Aspen

A quaint Victorian Gothic sofa dresses for today with its stripped wood and sleek black-velvet upholstery. Along with miniature turn-of-the-century twig furniture on the windowsill, the sofa gives this contemporary rustic gallery entrance an appealingly eccentric personality.
Design: Keith Monda; Photo: Rob Karosis

Still as he left it, the entrance to American march king
John Philip Sousa's home leads through a muted inter-
play of Victorian patterns, delicate woodwork, and
eclectic art into the crescendo of wallpaper, borders,
moldings, chandelier, and luxuries in the salon beyond.
Design: Anne Gozo; Photo: Bill Rothschild

Pineapple finials—nineteenth-century symbols of both hospitality and solid finances—punctuate a masterfully swept stairway. Tall, dark Victorian Gothic chairs with turnings and animal-head armrests mingle with lighter English-country hallway classics such as sporting paintings and Chinese Chippendale seating. Design: Martin Kuckly, Kuckly Associates, Inc.; Photo; Bill Rothschild

Greeting with flowers and sunny yellow hues, this entrance revels in such Victorian favorites as botanical prints, miniature topiary, and miniature furniture as well as plenty of floral chintz and needlepoint accessories. Design: Ellen Lemer; Photo: Bill Rothschild

The Victorian captivation with the Far East comes glowingly alive here with the kind of exuberant palettes and extraordinary lighting effects we love today. The chinoiserie bridge motif of the peach-and-green wallpaper, the Oriental bamboo hall table, the zigzag pleats, colorful decoupage, and spherical lamps exude a warm and effusive greeting in this foyer that is as cross-culturally young as it is evocatively elegant. Design: Tonin MacCallum; Photo: © image/dennis krukowski

Against a medieval-inspired wall treatment, an outstanding example of a neo-Gothic fruitwood secretary is flanked by a baroque cherub waving gilded lillies and announcing right there in the vestibule that the apartment develops heady Victorian themes throughout. Design: Albert Pensis; Photo: Bill Rothschild

A diverting example of Victoriana Mexicana makes this a one-of-a-kind passageway into a highly unusual nineteenth-century house. Angles and curves deftly play off each other as the dainty antique caned-and-curved settee and chairs hold their own along the spiral stairs, lofty wall moldings, massive billiard table, and colorful pyramid-shaped lamps. Photo: Tim Street-Porter

The entrance becomes a secret floating garden in this
breathtaking California transit between the main door
and the reception room, harboring much romance and
love of nature in a melding of late-Victorian, early Arts
and Crafts, and Japanese design aesthetics. Design:
Greene & Greene Architects; Photo: Tim Street-Porter

All the passionately held tenets of the Arts and Crafts Movement, especially the frame-
and-panel construction and the exquisite austerity of line, come together in this dazzling
cherry-wood and stained-glass California entrance. Beautiful cross-hatched beams on
the ceiling, spectacular Oriental rugs on the floor, as well as the stunning Mission lamp
and rare Craftsman-style piano make entering this home a unique artistic experience.
Design: Greene & Greene Architects; Photo: Tim Street-Porter

The late-Victorian era's appreciation of the beauty of nature manifested itself not only in glorious gardens but also indoors. The lacy, golden-fantasy tree motif on the glass panes of the beautiful wooden portal and paneled hallway hint of the coming Arts and Crafts Movement. Design: Greene & Greene Architects; Photo: Tim Street-Porter

Pressed-tin walls along the stairs—with their subtle texture and unmistakable Victorian reference—are left intact and glazed a rich burgundy, which makes a delightful color contrast to the lavender paint of the rest of the hallway. All this, along with the dramatic placement of the monumental lilly border, play up the superb craftsmanship of the woodwork. Design: Miller-Stein; Photo: David Duncan Livingston

The doors fling open to reveal one magical chamber after another full of Victorian romantic effects: a jewel-toned tufted duena settee in the center, a series of delicately upholstered chairs abloom with roses, and chandeliers that give a dazzling yet fragile impression. Photo: Tim Street-Porter

A sense of luxury and mystery drifts between these two tall, ambitiously carved nineteenth-century entrance doors. The experience of potentially passing through them holds an ineluctable anticipatory excitement. Their slightly strange scale yet loveliness of texture promise beautiful surprises and sensory delights. Photo: Tim Street-Porter

Piece by Piece *Entrance details*

While an authentic Victorian staircase should, by all means, be indulged with paint, wallpaper or wondrous lighting fixtures reminiscent of gaslit times, few homes today have the size and sweep of the original Victorian hallway. Still, the Victorian knack for reassuring arrivals and welcoming abundance can be enthrallingly captured with a few deft design touches. One or two unique period pieces can breathe warmth, charm, and character into even the smallest of entry areas. Try a cast-iron hall tree, a drop-leaf Sutherland table, an Oriental bamboo umbrella stand or a solitary Gothic chair with a peaked back full of whirligigs.

American Gingerbread

Though many of the nineteenth-century plains farm houses with their airy gingerbread porches have long been taken by time and wind, the tradition of a trelliswork enclosed point of entry or bright white wraparound porch still stands. This ever-fresh American welcome can be achieved through decorative wooden detailing on screen doors, porch posts, brackets, spandrels and gingerbread gables.

The Victorian Hallstand

If there is a single piece of furniture that can imbue the smallest foyer or the biggest reception hall with a Victorian aura, it is the visually enchanting hall tree. It comes in infinite varieties: from delicate English Oriental bamboo to overscaled Mid-Victorian American Gothic walnut constructions complete with boxtop compartments, seating, mirror and drip pans for walking sticks and umbrellas. Victorian Western-style receptacles extend pegs for cowboy hats and boots.

Say It with Flowers

Flowers and miniature topiary in the entry passageway epitomize the nature-loving Victorian attitude to prettiness and plentitude. Planters, jardiniers, cornucopias, botanical prints and jungly exotic potted palms enliven any room meant to receive guests after the front door is unlocked.

Western Victoriana

Since much of the mythic West and its material legacy have their source in the Victorian era, the buckskin and beads associated with cowboys and Indians, lawmen and outlaws work well in the entryway of ski houses and country houses with beaded wainscoting and log cabin architectural effects. Lassos, chaps, and Native American art bring terrific historic texture into a busy passageway without taking up much space.

The principle of unity between a room and its content was very much in vogue in Victorian times; therefore, the relationship between furniture and wallpaper was crucial. Arabesque paisleys, stylized florals, burgundy flocking and scenic Chinese vignettes often helped pull together a hallway's organized clutter. Stenciling, block-printing, carved woodpaneling and clubby leather wallcoverings did the same.

Lucent Loveliness

Dazzling balloon-glass chandeliers, fancifully formed brass sconces or free-standing cast-iron lamps did a lot to make the Victorian entrance glow with hospitality and a grand festive mood. Many of the old-fashioned gaslight designs of swirling brass and whirling bronze with rosy opaque, fluted, etched or leaded favrile glass shades are today widely available in both antique and reproduced versions.

Prelude to Romance

Wicker chairs and rockers, with their airy sculpted feeling and lighthearted evocation of lazy summer afternoons on an American porch or in an English cottage garden extend both refreshing greeting and an invitation to sit down. Above all, they perpetuate the Victorian ardor for bringing the outdoors in.

Stained-Glass Magic

Undulating tree motifs, bursts of brilliant Tiffany irises and water lillies, colorful Gothic church-style window inserts and translucent Art Nouveau lamps all add surprise and engrossing detail in an entrance way. Victorians used their powerful and painterly effects to create an uncanny range of serendipitous delights to make lasting first impressions on their guests.

Victorian
Living Rooms

The pliant, sink-into comfort of upholstered seating we love today and the ambient elegance of soft, attractive pillows casually strewn about living rooms were introduced to the English-speaking world in the Victorian parlor. So were high-definition windows and exotic trimmings.

 During the Victorian era, which partially overlapped in America with the unabashed richness of the Gilded Age, decorating became the ultimate indicator of social status. Nowhere was this craving for the cachet of stylish, novel, and expensive material goods more in evidence than in the most public room of the home—the formal salon. Opulent pattern was everywhere. Wallpapers, pottery, furniture, and stained-glass lamps were covered with lavish motifs.

The Victorian parlor gave birth to an astonishing variety of soft furniture, artful embellishment, and occasional tables used for tea and games. The round, button-tufted conversation settee, as well as the padded ottoman, cushiony Chesterfields with ends that could be adjusted to any angle for use as impromptu beds, Morris chairs and slipper chairs, delightful fabric-lavished round puffs, needlepoint covered footrests, prie-dieu chairs and rockers upholstered in Berlin-beaded tapestry, and especially the curvaceous sofas of the age—all of these items have gained favor in recent years. Of course, the wood-framed Victorian drawing room chairs with padded armrests possess eternal charm. So do whatnots—little unmatched tables, with layers of square or circular surfaces for the

display of treasured ornamental objects, and gypsy tables—scalloped, oval-top, fringed occasional tables with bobbin-turned tripod supports; as well as drop-leaf Sutherland hunt tables, and the endless variations of Oriental bamboo side tables, folding screens, whimsically constructed breakfronts and serpentine wall stands.

Naturally, some the artsy-craftsy knickknacks fashioned by hobby-loving Victorian women— such as wax-flower and seashell assemblages under glass domes—are harder to integrate into the way we now live. Today, the heavy-handed Renaissance Revival furniture and baroque bibelots seem ponderous and cloying.

When bringing the Victorian spirit into the living room, we need a fresh perspective on the Victorian parlor. Its admirable sense of volume can be best captured by lovely Arabian rugs, elaborate window treatments, and such anchors as a stunning sofa and a firescreen-embellished fireplace. Understanding the visual complexity of a decorating scheme, it is possible to appreciate that even an elaborately wrought, mother-of-pearl inlaid Victorian papier-mâché piece has to stand on its own legs, so to speak, nowadays. Pulled out of its original environment it can grace—as can the most curlicued Gothic Revival chair—even minimalist loftspace.

This high-ceilinged room incorporates furniture and art from three centuries into a stylish living area done in soothing green and cream. A shawl draped asymmetrically over wood-slat window blinds fits in with the easygoing ambiance.
Design: Mark Epstein; Photo: Peter Peirce

Before the age of television the piano was the focus of leisure hours and social life in many American homes. In this genteel living room, the nineteenth-century affinity for flowered fabrics and ornate, tasseled draperies is interpreted in soft colors for modern sensibilities.
Design: James Coursey, Coursey Design Consultants ; Photo: Rob Karosis

A single, eccentric Victorian element such as a canopied leather chair makes any room memorable. White walls provide a clean backdrop for a rich layering of carpets and fabrics.
Design: McMillen Inc.; Photo: Bill Rothschild

Victorian-inspired rooms run the gamut from casual, creative interpretations to historically correct renditions of period style such as this living room with a charming bay window. Each design element is selected for authenticity as well as aesthetic appeal, such as the red-and-green color scheme that was inspired by a mid- to late-nineteenth-century color theory advocating harmony of contrasts. The beaded, ebonized card table and chairs form beautiful silhouettes as sunlight streams in the windows. Design: Bill and Arlene Schwind; Photo: Rob Karosis

In a contemporary take on Victorian elements, a monochromatic palette and restrained selection of objects showcase strong nineteenth-century forms and textures: the scroll-ended sofa, lustrous wicker armchairs and coffee table, and revivalist caned chair with twist turnings inspired by the era of Charles II. Design: Marcy Balk; Photo: Peter Peirce

Rosy-hued stripes and flowers team up to establish a refined, upbeat mood in this lovely coastal manor, where it's easy to imagine reading the morning paper over coffee while waiting for the sun to warm the beach outdoors. Design: Gary McBournie; Photo: Steve Vierra

Victorians were fascinated with objects from places far beyond the Western world. In this pretty room, that fascination comes through in a distinctly Indian birdcage harkening back to the time of the Raj, and the blue and white fabrics and wallcoverings reminiscent of designs on Chinese export porcelain. Design: Gail Greene; Photo: Bill Rothschild

Victorian design was exported from England all over the world, mixing with the indigenous styles of various countries. In a Mexican hacienda, the dark, refined finish of high-style upholstered seating contrasts with the house's pale, unpolished flooring and woodwork. Photos: Tim Street-Porter

A genuine Victorian parlor illustrates the mid-century predilection for combining colorful and highly patterned carpets, upholstery fabrics, and wallcoverings. True to the era's style, the walls are papered with a decorative border wrapping around the top of the room.
Photo: David Duncan Livingston

By the middle of the nineteenth century, center tables were in vogue in the opulently bordered rooms where families received guests. In today's rooms that allude to Victorian style without attempting historical accuracy, the modern-day equivalent of the center table—the lower-height coffee table—is perfectly acceptable. Photo: David Duncan Livingston

By the end of the nineteenth century, animal skins were the rage for floors in parlors and libraries. Many modern decorators, while tending to eschew the real thing, have fun with imitation patterns such as leopard-skin carpet. This interior's lively spirit continues with rich coloring, a stylized oval-backed wooden chair and settee, and the walls' regiment of golden stars lined up in perfect formation. Design: Robert Fiegal; Photos: David Duncan Livingston

An idiosyncratic, three-sided upholstered chair designed for a courting couple and a chaperone draws the attention of everyone who enters the room. In Victorian homes with massive living areas, establish strong focal points such unique furniture, massive artwork, or rugs with large-scale patterns to serve as visual anchors. Design: David Barrett; Photo: Bill Rothschild

Windows became larger and more plentiful during the nineteenth century, not only because Victorians believed that rooms filled with light and air were healthier, but also due to new availability of large, plate-glass, sash windows. The Roman shades shown here are a close cousin of the Venetian curtains of the era. Photo: Dave Marlow/Aspen

A single dramatic alabaster bust—the kind Victorians crowded in multitudes into their front parlors—oversees this relaxedly live-able but decidedly romantic living room. Its sunny balloon window shades, comforting plants, throws, and pillows spin around the room's two other decorative focal points—the shapely iron daybed and the mirror-topped marble fireplace. Design: Louis Navarrete, Bobbi Henley, and Victoria Pasko; Photo: Tony Giammarino

The Victorians were fascinated with wallpapers, made prevalent use of wainscoting, and showed great fondness for spindly Oriental bamboo furniture. All this is invitingly reinterpreted in a summer-fresh seaside living room of today. Design: Mark Hampton; Photo: Stan Rumbough

A large white bookcase with a graceful pediment oversees this formal living room that manages a joyful aura of immediacy while savoring such popular examples of Victoriana as classical busts and figurines, a Gothic Revival chair, and gilt mirrors and furniture. Extensive use of white in fabrics and painted furniture keeps deep-brown walls from seeming somber. Design: Mark Hampton; Photo: Stan Rumbough

In a very special interior guaranteed to raise one's spirits, an extensive collection of yellow and blue porcelain with Oriental themes acts as a catalyst for the entire room, with similar patterns and colors carried through fabrics and other decorative elements. When collections are put together in tight groupings, such as ceramic items or a gathering of family photographs, the effect is unified and orderly rather than cluttered. Photo: © image/dennis krukowski

In romantic, modern-day interpretations of Victorian ambiance, ivory-painted walls, ceilings, and woodwork often serve as an unobtrusive backdrop for fabrics and colors that complement rather than contrast with one another. Cabbage roses, such as those seen in the fabric covering the sofa and draped at the windows, were one of Queen Victoria's favorite design motifs. Design: Carol O'Brien and Susan Harris, Wellesley Design Consultants; Photo: Steve Vierra

Four unique armchairs, with graphic, sinuous curves and powdery-blue moiré upholstery, gather around a contemporary coffee table with the confident posturing of key executives at a board meeting. When furniture groupings are tightened like this, conversations tend to be more focused and intense. Photo: Tim Street-Porter

Modestly scaled furniture drawn together in a tight conversational grouping keeps this inviting yet relatively small parlor from seeming overcrowded. Colors and patterns also are edited for an open, airy ambiance. Design: Karen Day; Photo: Dave Marlow/Aspen

An asymmetrical approach to the sofa design, window treatment, and furniture layout make this small parlor less stiff and formal. The large palm is an essential element of the room, just as houseplants often were in Victorian times. Design: Leighton Candler; Photo: Bill Rothschild

Borders and fringes are an integral part of Victorian flair, extending in this Scottish-flavored room to such painstaking details as braiding applied beneath the encircling cornice. An upholstered settee is transformed into a sofa by a clever back cushion suspended from a rod hung on the wall. Design: Robert Clark + Raymond LeCuyer; Photo: Bill Rothschild

Regardless of the weather outside, this delightful parlor always glows with the warmth of its red walls and rug. The blue of Chinese export porcelain and other accents stands in cooling contrast, while floral slipcovers and a fancy needlework tablecloth keep the Victorian cottage ambiance soft and thoroughly charming. Design: Tonin MacCallum; Photos: © image/dennis krukowski

Victorian style ranges from the full, busy rooms commonly associated with the period, to those with a less-cluttered look we prefer today. With just a few well-chosen pieces of nineteenth-century furniture, such as this stunning Gothic-framed sofa and English long-case clock, as well as some joyous floral fabric, the era's exquisite charms come through without any sense of fussiness. Design: Ben Theodore; Photo: Steve Vierra

Tented rooms seem like surreal hideaways in the midst of a sultry foreign land. The exotic atmosphere is heightened here by wonderful furniture and fabrics that celebrate the visually enriching Victorian adventures encountered beyond England and the European continent. Design: McMillen Inc.; Photo: Bill Rothschild

By the final decades of the nineteenth century, machine-made furniture and overwrought decoration met opposition in the form of the Arts and Crafts Movement. These rooms stand in refreshing pared-down contrast to the fussy design so popular with the newly monied who cluttered everything with masses of material objects, testimony of their success. Bypassing frills and ornate carving in favor of rectilinear architectural forms and unadorned handcrafted furniture with graceful proportions. Photos: Tim Street-Porter

Tapestry-woven upholstery with geometric patterns brings exotic flavor to the living room of the Colgate house in Litchfield, where the inspiration of the Arts and Crafts Movement is strongly felt. Daylight glows through brightly colored panes of glass, casting a warm glow on the decor's russets and earth tones. Design: Alvin Schneider; Photo: Bill Rothschild

The nature-oriented American Victorians enjoyed the concept of rusticating in the great outdoors, an idea picked up on in this upstate New York getaway, which is an ode to hunting and fishing. The small Saranac Lake boat-turned-hutch is a whimsical addition. Design: Robert DeCarlo and Jonathon Kusa; Photo: © image/Dennis Krukowski

Audacious and energizing, a striking red room is redolent with pattern and saturated with color from floor to ceiling. Spending time here is like basking in the warm glow of a fire's red flames. Design: David Barrett; Photo: Bill Rothschild

U.S. President Theodore Roosevelt was reputed to be a formidable hunter of wild game, a hobby attested to by the trophies on display in his late-nineteenth-century home on New York's Long Island. Considering the Victorians' fascination with rare items and the natural world, it's no surprise that decorating with real animal skins was a status symbol. Photo: Bill Rothschild, Courtesy of National Park Service

Piece by Piece *Living Room*
details

Designing Victorian living rooms requires juggling dozens of details while keeping the big picture in mind—thinking about everything from a needlepoint pillow and a sofa's fringe, to establishing the powerful focal points needed to provide order and rhythm in rooms characterized by abundance. In the course of putting it all together and taking cues from the denizens of the nineteenth century, remember to infuse the room with your own personality, whether through such collectibles as whatnots or settees, the books on display, or the colors you choose to be surrounded by.

Hearths with Heart

The Victorians decorated fireplaces as exuberantly as everything else in their living rooms, using mantels to display favorite objects and even to hang drapery from. Then, as now, placing a splendid painting or mirror above the mantel draws further attention, reinforcing the idea that the hearth is heart of the home.

Design: Emma Eckelberry; Photo: Bill Rothschild

Design: Emma Eckelberry; Photo: Bill Rothschild

Up Against the Wall

Wall and ceiling papers had a heyday during Victoria's reign, and today numerous sources offer genuine period borders and papers incorporating themes of the day such as exotic locales and floral motifs.

Touches of Needlework

All kinds of needlework—embroidery, crocheting, and needlepoint—harken back to the time when ladies of leisure honed their domestic skills during quiet evenings in the parlor. Needlepoint pillows and upholstery continue to be favorites in today's nostalgic homes.

All the Trimmings

Detail living room furniture and pillows with fringe, braiding, and tassels, decorating everything including the family pet's wicker bed. Spaniels, incidentally, were beloved by Queen Victoria.

Design: Emma Eckelberry; Photo: Bill Rothschild

Windows to the World

Parlor window treatments range from historically accurate versions such as complex, multi-layered draperies or fringed valances on top of lace panels, to more contemporary approaches such as loosely hung draperies with a less studied appearance.

Design: Camille Belmonte and Mary Beth Galvin, Wellesley Design Center; Photo: Steve Vierra

Design: Jessica Flynn; Photo: Steve Vierra

Victorian Dining Areas

It is nearly impossible to imagine any festive celebration of today without the delicious magic, heart-warming ornamentation, and nearly novelistic riches of bright and buoyant minutiae that originated in the radiant Victorian dining room.

Picture an airy chiffonier—the prettily proportioned, heightened Victorian sideboard—turning into a poetic still life with an antique lace runner, a sparkling cut-crystal vase filled with a bouquet of white lilacs, a delicate set of bone china teacups and saucers, and a silver platter holding a white-iced christening cake. Or think of the classic Dickensian Christmas. A dozen fine-formed chairs pulled around an opulently decked oblong table, as turkey or goose and a multitude of covered or heaped vegetable dishes blend a familiar aroma that insidiously insinuates itself into our nostrils. The room is wreathed all around not only by lushly colored wallpaper, but also by garlands of green boughs gaily wrapped with red ribbons. These hang from the upper moldings, festoon the fireplace and windows. Sometimes the evergreens entwine with strings of holly berries and popcorn or mat a side table weighted with pies and cookies, perhaps a charming home-baked gingerbread house or a lovingly prepared English plum pudding. Amazingly, every one of these holiday concepts first came to life during the Victorian era.

Though emerald green and ruby red are authentic Victorian color schemes and red-flocked damask walls are instant mental images of nineteenth-century dining rooms, a whole gamut of blush-pale hues, not to speak of Chinese-inspired murals, Japanese screens, and meticulously crafted wood-paneling jeweled with stained glass, all tap into the plentitudinous well of Victorian dining ambiance. The pastiche of styles and embellishments, the wide range of revivals—Gothic, Greek, Rococo—all culminated in the Victorian dining room. Home entertaining, table settings, and food presentation reflected the exuberant synthesis of aesthetics. A successful dinner party was a social indicator, giving one developed into an art form.

The Victorian belief in the principle of harmony between a house and its content was particularly evident in the dining room, where it throws interesting sidelights on the social implications of the Victorian design stratification of cottage, farm, and villa. The cottager's sideboard was seldom painted and usually made of deal. It was often called a dresser and held ceramic dishes. Housewives kept them snowy white by scouring their surfaces with fine sand. In old farmhouses, sideboards were made of oak rubbed bright. These featured shelves filled with rows of pewter plates polished to look like silver. In the shining dining rooms of British aristocrats, splendid mahogany sideboards were set out with gold and silver pieces. Wealthy New World merchants, silver kings, and cattle barons were quick to adapt this and other fancy accoutrements of the Victorian English and Scottish baronial dining room. They especially imitated complex recessed ceilings, glowingly magnificent overhead and side lighting, layer upon layer of Oriental rugs, and many Elizabethan and Gothic flourishes associated with royalty and the church.

Updated Victorian style can be ravishingly romantic and utterly uplifting. Painted dining chairs, and glorious fabrics used in generous amounts and on a multitude of soft pillows are a perfect antidote to our hard-edged, high-tech age.
Design: John Ryman; Photo: Stewart O'Shields

A bay of windows crowned with a pentagonal, leaded-glass window lets light flood into this attractive room. The seating, all upholstered with blue velvet, represents two nineteenth-century revivalist styles: one pair of chairs is in the style of Charles I and II (referred to by the Victorians as Elizabethan Revival), while those partially visible on the right and left are Rococo Revival. Design: Richard and Patricia Kent with Ron Kanan; Photo: Dave Marlow/Aspen

A complementary color scheme featuring melon-orange walls and the blue of a porcelain collection animates this luscious dining room. The wall color and border extend onto the beams, incorporating the ceiling into the design. Design: Tonin MacCallum; Photo: © image/dennis krukowski

Roses—the quintessential Victorian flower—fill a porcelain, Chinese-theme tureen that serves as a centerpiece in this delightful spot for champagne brunch. The round table encourages intimate conversation, meandering along as the morning unfolds. Furniture and Fabrics by Summer Hill Ltd.

With cut crystal glittering on the chandelier and wall fixtures, gold accents on dishes and glassware, and a vintage embroidered-linen tablecloth, this seaside room offers a sophisticated, more-formal dining experience. The cornice has been painted in subtle colors similar to those on the chairs and screen. Design: Manijeh M. Emery, M. M. Interiors; Photo: Steve Vierra

Curvaceous Victorian iron chairs, a round little period table, and a collection of blue and white plates and porcelain objects provide the theme for this two-tone dining area, where the genial atmosphere makes a perfect pick-me-up setting for afternoon tea and crumpets. Design: Bennett & Judie Weinstock Interiors, Inc.; Photo: © image/dennis krukowski

Victorian romanticism takes on a soft country air with a blue-and-cream color scheme that runs consistently through the table linens, upholstery, window treatment, and wallpaper. Photo courtesy of Waverly

In an idyllic country setting, this jaunty dining area, full of stripes and flowers, provides an optimistic start to the day. Woodwork highlighted by a border with a colorful twist-turn pattern is just one of the details that adds up to a Victorian look. Photo courtesy of Waverly

In lieu of a carpet, a floor painted to look like a rug is easy to clean while still establishing a distinct sense of place. The effect is polished and lighthearted, underlining the whimsical nature of the marble-topped Victorian buffet and the stained glass wall insert. Design: Lois Weir; Photo: Tony Giammarino

Lush bouquets of fresh flowers, including an idiosyncratic tiered tower punctuated with yellow tulips, echo the sentiments of the floral wallpaper. Stripes and flowers always make a happy marriage, as in the fringed square of fabric placed over a floral under cloth. Design: Marshall Watson; Photo: Mick Hales of Greenworld Pictures

Knowing where to put color in a period room so as to emphasize pleasing architectural elements is illustrated by this colorful Victorian border which rounds the bay window to create an alternate dining area for one-on-one repasts. The table for two in this corner of the living room is intimate yet part of the embellishment of the larger space, color-cued to the tufted sofa of yellow silk. Design: Terry Pieciak; Photo: Steve Vierra

Wainscoting brings a classic Victorian look to this richly decorated dining room in a restored Italianate house. The floral motif in the historic wallpaper is an example of Egyptian Revival style, which was sparked by the opening of the Suez Canal in 1869. Today, the paper's design is as beautiful as ever, while continuing to speak eloquently of the excitement surrounding one of the great events of the nineteenth century. Design: Bill and Arlene Schwind; Photo: Rob Karosis

Woodwork is a key element in this formal dining room in a Victorian house, with paneled wainscoting extending up two-thirds of the wall, a simplified look that emerged late in the century. Painted white, the wainscoting offers a clean backdrop that emphasizes the silhouettes of late-eighteenth-century shield-back chairs. Design: Kathy Best, Photo: David Duncan Livingston

Dining rooms, with their relatively spare furnishings, are great places to showcase the flamboyant wallpapers, borders, and ceiling designs of the nineteenth century. The sunflowers and sunbursts featured here were popular motifs of the fanciful look the Victorians referred to as Queen Anne style. Photo: David Duncan Livingston

Dining room tables often do double duty as a study or library table. A lamp, such as this fringed brass one, adds style and offers task lighting for a range of activities, from eating to reading to writing. Design: Stephanie Stokes; Photo: © image/dennis krukowski

The enveloped, protected feeling that dark-paneled walls bring to a room is amplified by the brown ceiling and shaded coloring of the rug and upholstery. After nightfall, subtle recessed lighting and candle flames create a welcoming, seductive glow amid the darkness. Design: Faye Etter Interior Design; Photo: Steve Vierra

Victorians took immense pride in giving dinner parties and set the stage for these festive special occasions with a passion for all the arts involved. Textiles, porcelain, and glass were used to provoke vibrancy between a room's furniture and art-decked walls. High-back, ornately covered upholstered dining chairs encircled long formal tables with a cohesive bracket of warming sociability. Design: Joe and Hargi Hemingway; Photo: Tony Giammarino

Pairing highly detailed wallpaper and patterned carpet satisfies modern-day design sensibilities when the colors harmonize beautifully such as these. Balloon-back chairs, so called because their shape resembles that of a hot-air balloon, were extremely popular in the mid-nineteenth century. Photos: David Duncan Livingston

Windows opening to an unsurpassable mountain view are adorned
only with simple shades to maximize the view and to fit agreeably
with the rustic Western interpretation of a Victorian aesthetic. For
mealtimes with a casual, comfortable ambiance, mix and match
dining chairs and even include upholstered easy chairs. Design:
Lipkin Warner Design + Planning; Photo: Dave Marlow

Today, many houses with grand Victorian-style architecture are furnished with pieces from various design eras. Here, the
Windsor chairs and trestle table reference earlier centuries, but their rich, burnished wooden surfaces fit in perfectly with
the room's woodwork. Design: Miller Stein; Photo: David Duncan Livingston

Bare floors are a cool option for sultry climates. This soaring dining room in a Mexican hacienda, where North American Victoriana found a uniquely imaginative form of expression, features a striking inlaid floor with a central pattern and border evocative of a rug. Photo: Tim Street-Porter

Although designers associated with the Arts and Crafts Movement eschewed excessive ornamentation, they lavished attention on simple, subtle elements such as the ebonized detailing in the dining table, chairs, and buffets in this exquisite period house. Glasswork in the light fixtures and cabinet doors also attains the level of art in this refreshing, exquisitely crafted dining room. Design: Greene & Greene Architects; Photos: Tim Street-Porter

Even when a house's architecture isn't nineteenth century, a Victorian ambiance can be cultivated with a few well-thought-out touches. In this dining room, an air of romanticism arises from a painted screen, caned chairs, old-time varieties of fresh flowers, and porcelain figures of dogs and cats.
Design: Teri Seidman; Photo: Bill Rothschild

Austerity was unknown when it came to the Victorian dining room. New standards of ostentatious propriety set sideboards aglow with resplendent ruby-red decanters and colorful glass stemware. Lavish use of silver and the extravagant multi-color of shimmering Tiffany lamps still bring startling effects into contemporary lives that echo with Victorian textural interest.
Design: Cynthia and David Robinson; Photo: Tony Giammarino

With an eclecticism nearly as far-reaching as that embraced by the Victorians, this massive dining room in a grand historic house brings together heirlooms from various periods. Among the quintessentially Victorian-era highlights: woodwork that has been grained, marbleized, and decorated with other special paint treatments. Design: Robert Clark + Raymond LeCuyer; Photos: Bill Rothschild

Taking the well-crafted and witty best of Victorian forms and marrying them to the light-filled, casual, multi-pur-
pose decorating philosophy of today succeeds in this varied blend of curving and straight, sensuous and simple
good lines. This is epitomized by the inventive detail and inherent fantasy of the authentic nineteenth-century
folding screen and newly minted outdoorsy chairs. Design: Christine McCabe; Photo: Tony Giammarino

The sumptuous apex of Victorian indulgence in collecting fruit-and-flower motif porcelain was the display in the dining room vitrine. In this atmosphere-rich recreation of how an impressive collection of antique Limoges plates can
imbue a room with Victorian color and spirit, an elaborate crystal icicle-rimmed chandelier, a precious old lace table
cloth and abundantly carved, caned Renaissance Revival chairs all play an important part. Design: Carol Ann
Germano; Photo: Tony Giammarino

A pair of rose-colored upholstered chairs and a tea table near the window add another dimension to this tradition-minded dining room, which is also enhanced by an elegant buffet and built-in shelving. The room's proportions are generous enough to accommodate the ample chandelier and the pervasive presence of an ancestral portrait. Design: Marshall Watson and Adair Matthews; Photo: Billy Cunningham

Dining Area
details

Dining rooms are ideal venues for playing out everyone's fantasies about the Victorian era as a time when well-mannered, proper ladies and gentlemen took pleasure in genteel pastimes and refined company. The well-thought-out selection of major dining-room elements such as the table, chairs, chandelier, and wall and floor coverings is vital. But the little things make a big difference, too. Indeed, those minor details—bouquets of teeming roses, delicate china and glassware, linens lovingly embroidered or edged with lace, pretty ribbons tied around folded napkins—all add up to major vintage style.

Design: Shane Miller; Photo: Tony Giammarino

Linens and Lace
Fresh table linens, whether vintage cloths discovered in an antique shop, new fabrics with old-time flair, or both layered together, are essential for dressed-up Victorian dining rooms. For lighter, more informal meals, use linen or lace place mats rather than a full-size cloth.

The Victorians were great collectors, never missing an opportunity to prominently display beloved objects such as porcelain or glassware. To augment a collection and create a coordinated dining area, let the themes and colors of a cherished collection drive the design of the entire room.
Design: Mark Hampton; Photo: Stan Rumbough

Everything in Its Place

Set the dining table as if creating a work of art, paying attention to fine points such as the layering of plates and the artful presentation of napkins. Each element included in a place setting, from the china or ceramic plates to the cut-glass goblets or hand-blown glasses, contributes to an air of formality or informality.

Design: Teri Seidman; Photo: Bill Rothschild

Hearts and Flowers

Colorful flowers add instant romance to any dining room, whether arranged as a lush centerpiece for the table or fashioned into a sweet arrangement for an adjacent sideboard or pedestal.

On the Side

A buffet or sideboard adjacent to the table comes in handy for serving and storage. Choose from traditional pieces in dark woods or, for new Victorian style, a buffet that combines nineteenth-century styling with the freshness of white paint.

Victorian
Kitchens

Surely, no room is more aptly suited to the generous menu of Victorian decor than the one where we nurture, create, and gather family and friends. A kitchen may be redolent of bay leaf and thyme, earthy soup and fresh-baked bread, but what can really breathe it full of bustling warmth and cottagey whimsy is an exuberance of visual detail evocative of the dailiness of Victorian life.

Surrounded as we are at work and at home by efficient but impersonal technological marvels, when it comes to the kitchen, we increasingly savor the human touch. Digitally programmed appliances may do a lot of the sizzling, simmering, and whirring these days; but in a space we fondly think of as the heart of the home, we yearn for design that's emotionally engaging and flavorfully personal. Happily, a staggering array of available culinary miscellanea from the Victorian era is vibrantly endowed with exactly that kind of ambiance-making power. Leaf-chased tankards and woodland-glazed teapots, Georgia pine work tables and brass-ornamented cupboards are virtual ledgers of family histories. Eye-catching doorstops and amusing bootscrapers—some shaped like domestic or exotic animals—are full of references to the tumultuous outpouring of distinctive and eclectic nineteenth-century inventiveness and craftsmanship. Many of the then newly mass-produced yet elaborately wrought storage units, fancy fluted light fixtures, and twirly cast-iron furnishings are endearingly iconographic of the fun status symbols of an aspiring middle class on both sides of the Atlantic. Myriad odd finds from the era can build a richness of textural echo into a spacious L-shaped family kitchen or endow a slimly efficient apartment cooking spot with a delightfully customized and inhabited feeling.

Of course, amply cluttered and well-equipped as the original Victorian kitchen was, it functioned decades before the discovery of electricity, not to speak of electronics. The Victorian larder, with its cool slate floors that kept food from spoiling, was the equivalent of our refrigerator and pantry. There was also the scullery, an area used not only for scraping produce but also for washing dishes and table linens. As we do today, Victorians sometimes liked to bask in the snug charms of the kitchen. This was especially true of North America. At the end of a long, active day outdoors, everyone in the household gravitated around one of those big, wonderful, wooden work tables centered in farmhouse kitchens all across the vast, windswept plains. Another popular contemporary kitchen attraction—the large pubby clock—was already a Victorian favorite.

Today's Victorian kitchen need not be dark or heavy-laden. To summon an enriched backdrop for many of the high-tech conveniences that draw us there for increasingly longer hours on evenings and weekends, we need not go back to anything impractical. Carefully applied ornamentation can supply the coziness of long ago without sacrificing up-to-the-minute microwaves and refrigerators. Beaded wainscoting, pressed-tin ceilings, stenciled botanical borders, tiled walls and floors, glass-paneled cabinetry, ceramic knobs, brass faucets, and overhead bric-a-brac are but a few means to imbue a kitchen with the patina and panache of the past.

A light and airy California kitchen in pale, buttery hues carries the torch for both angular Arts and Crafts motifs such as the light fixtures and curvy, warm Victorian botanical themes. Design: Julie Atwood; Photos: David Duncan Livingston

New Victorian interiors are often light and airy, as evidenced by this delightful kitchen in pale buttery hues. The decorative frieze encircling the room on the upper walls is a lilting interpretation of the botanical themes so popular after the 1870s. Dark woodwork, echoed here in the floor inlay and central table, is another vestige of the century.
Design: Julie Atwood; Photos: David Duncan Livingston

Oversize crown moldings and soffits with dentil trim result in a formal look appropriate to stately nineteenth-century homes. The chairs at the dining table and island eating area are made to look like bamboo, a popular furniture motif during Victoria's reign. Photo courtesy of Canac Kitchens

Numerous intense colors and complementary combinations, appreciated for their ability to set just the right mood for specific room types, were in vogue during the nineteenth century. This kitchen's striking blue is a cheerful, cool color that is complemented by the warmer tones of the maple work surfaces and cocoa-colored floor. Design and photo: Mark Wilkinson Furniture, UK

This apple-green cottage kitchen, complete with period seating covered with floral, needlepoint upholstery, exudes a relaxed coziness that invites informal visits over tea at the timeworn table. The Victorians, with their love of abundance, would have appreciated the many touches of greenery, china, and glazed ceramic ware. Peach fabric hanging at the doorway is a lighter take on the heavy draperies called portières that helped reduce drafts in the 1800s. Photo: David Duncan Livingston

This charming kitchen takes its inspiration from the Arts and Crafts Movement, which stressed simple, handcrafted furniture in response to the heavily ornamented styles of the early to mid-nineteenth century. The cabinetry's hand-painted surfaces also are appropriate for Victorian rooms. Photo courtesy of Mark Wilkinson Furniture, UK

In keeping with the many ways nineteenth-century home-owners decoratively painted wooden surfaces, this kitchen benefits from a lively checkerboard floor pattern that lets the floorboards' grain show through. Pendant lights over the island strike a contemporary note, making this kitchen eclectic in a way that most likely would have pleased the Victorians, who were the ultimate fans of eclecticism. Design: Carol O'Brien and Susan Harris, Wellesley Design Consultants; Photo: Steve Vierra

Homey yellow-checked curtains and an antique table's golden patina bring warmth to this Victorian cottage kitchen. A built-in hutch with paned-glass cabinet fronts provides storage for glasses and plates as well as a handy buffet surface. Design: Tammy Couture; Photo: Steve Vierra

Today's kitchens often begin with a foundation of traditional style and then add an interesting twist. This cabinetry's natural pine finish, for instance, is an unexpected and refreshing alternative to the dark wood more common in **Victorian rooms.** Photo courtesy of Wood Mode and Kitchen Aid

True to the Victorian affinity for whimsy and faux surfaces, this kitchen features a delightful trompe l'oeil painting depicting a stone backsplash behind the range and a narrow shelf running beneath upper cabinets. Design and photo: Mark Wilkinson Furniture, UK

Many of today's Victorian kitchens incorporate contemporary appliances, but for a purer period look consider a new range with old-fashioned styling. This distinctive model fits seamlessly into its surroundings. Chairs with bentwood bases and fine-woven wicker seats are another nod to the era. Design and photo: Mark Wilkinson Furniture, UK

Wonderful white-washed Victorian-style woodwork refreshingly partitions the green-tiled and brightly wallpapered workzone from the more seriously antique-furnished but delightfully unpretentious dining area in this newly old-fashioned kitchen designed for easy socializing. Design: Gary Paul; Photo: © Image/dennis krukowski

A medley of honey-colored woods brings unmistakable warmth to this eat-in kitchen, where bead-board paneling makes appliances blend in with the cabinetry and walls. Reproduction pendant lighting and wall fixtures, electrified rather than fueled by the gas or oil typical of nineteenth-century lamps, retain an authentic flavor. Design: Karen Day; Photo: Dave Marlow/Aspehn

Versatility is designed into this high-ceilinged kitchen, with a large island for working and quick dining, a desk for taking care of business, a glass-front display cupboard, and a built-in unit along the windows for storage and buffet service. A deep shade of red infuses the walls with drama, while abundant white cabinetry and woodwork brighten the overall effect. Design: Monte Berkoff Kitchens; Photo: Bill Rothschild

This kitchen's windows are framed with greenery in a manner similar to a window curtained with plants, which was illustrated in *The American Woman's Home,* a guide to decorating written by Catherine Beecher and Harriet Beecher Stowe in 1869. Design: Florence Perchuk; Photo: Bill Rothschild, Photo courtesy of Kitchen Aid

A few well-chosen touches can infuse any room with period style. Here, antique birdcages, a floral needlepoint rug, and two types of plants favored by Victorians—African violets and topiaries—transform a new, white kitchen into a welcoming spot. Design: Lisa Bonneville; Photo: Steve Vierra

This chock-full kitchen, with its deep-cushioned wicker settee and cozy dining table, encourages friends and family to settle in for leisurely repasts. A massive cast-iron range provides a primary focal point, while a visual feast of patterns, plants, and jars of foodstuff fill in with decorative details. Design: Lee Napolitano; Photo: Bill Rothschild

The look of bounty, the feel of long-ago ricochets through this thickly atmospheric kitchen. Its Victorian-style windows, doorways, and cabinetry combined with vivid wallpaper, interesting containers for colorful produce, and especially the casually ornamented sideboard, turned central table and triad of fluted glass shades on a vintage brass chandelier transform this room from a more meal-preparation workshop into a family gathering center. Design: Gary Paul; Photo: © image dennis krukowski

Some of the most charming Victorian kitchens leave original elements such as cabinets, sinks, and flooring intact but enhanced by inexpensive solutions as basic as creative paint treatments. Here, for instance, homey gathered curtains conceal under-sink plumbing fittings and bring a uniform look to glass cabinet doors. Design: Rena Fortgang; Photo: Bill Rothschild

Small yet efficient and attractive, this kitchen emulates Victorian style with a black-and-white tile floor and heavily grained wooden cabinetry. Two types of upper cabinets are shown: open shelving for decorative pottery, and glass-front cabinets to keep more frequently used dishes and serving pieces free of dust and ready for use. Design: Anthony Antine; Photo: Bill Rothschild

Dark wooden cabinetry provides an ideal foil for a checkerboard floor and a colorful collection of majolica and other glazed pottery and porcelain. Huge quantities of majolica ware were distributed as premiums in the United States in the 1880s. Design: Judith Levithan and Michael Orsini; Photo: Bill Rothschild

Kitchen
details

While domesticity, industry, and simple objects in everyday use were exalted during Victorian times, the nineteenth-century kitchen lacked the flourishes of Victorian style. Today, though, the kitchen is the heart of the home, functioning not only as a practical center for preparing meals but also as a family room. Thus design elements formerly reserved for parlors and dining rooms—fine cabinetry, decorative flooring, charming fabrics, sophisticated paint treatments, and fascinating groupings of collectibles—are now essential considerations when planning Victorian-style kitchens.

A Push for Pulls

Old-style porcelain, crystal, and brass pulls for kitchen drawers and cabinets are among the little details that add up to Victorian style.
Design: Julie Atwood; Photos: David Duncan Livingston

Design: Lynn Robinson and Cecilia K. Wheeler; Photo: Bill Rothschild

The Victorians were known for decorating every surface in their homes, and many of today's kitchen cabinetry options continue that legacy with decorative paint treatments, intricate carving, or doors of paned, leaded, or beveled glass.

Under Foot

Wooden floors, while often stained and varnished, can be painted or dyed for a lively Victorian look. Tiles are another durable choice for period kitchens.

Petal Power

Create a fresh, romantic atmosphere by using plenty of flowers and plants—fresh, dried, or artistically rendered on fabrics, tiles, floors, or wallcoverings.

Victorian Bedrooms

The bedroom is a safe haven for our most intimate needs. It enfolds our soulful whispers and tender touches, snuggles and snores, hopes and dreams. Some of the most significant private experiences take place within its walls. Nightly, we retreat to its sheltering comforts for sleep, rest, and renewal. It is here that the Victorian spirit provides most amply what we so much crave today: an atmosphere laced with romance and cushioning mind-body repair.

Though bedroom styles changed drastically, both in England and America, during Queen Victoria's almost three-quarter-century reign, many of the nocturnal fineries we love to abandon ourselves to after a taxing day were already making their irresistible invitations during those years. Victorians knew the delights of climbing between embroidery-hemmed, fresh, white sheets. They taught us the pleasure of sinking our heads into depths of layered pillows and to take cover under button-tufted silk comforters in the city and patchwork quilts on the prairie.

The Victorian era glorified the bedroom with fantastical beds, momentous armoires—which they called wardrobes—and gargantuan floor-to-ceiling mirrors. Other sleeping-quarter embellishments included lovely tall windows dressed in soft and diaphanous fabrics, frilly dressing tables, handsome four-drawer chests, marble-topped nightstands, splendid writing desks, and such eccentric or exotic pieces for sitting as Turkish rockers, ambidexters, Chesterfields, davenports, and various quirky, curlicued occasional chairs.

In the early years of the period, the bed was indulged all around and to the floor with weighty woolen or silk-lined velvet drapery. Its purpose was to conserve warmth around the sleeper. By the mid-nineteenth century, the half-tester—with fabric to draw around only head and shoulders gained favor. So did the four-poster with a canopy of flouncy ruffles or a network of crocheting stretched overhead. Though privacy and practicality were middle Victorian concerns, the status impulse of the time was to copy the extravagantly ornamented beds of earlier historical periods, particularly the Italian Renaissance, Tudor England, and the courts at Versailles. The well-proportioned, classic English bedsteads of Chippendale, Sheraton, and Hepplewhite became overshadowed by powerful Gothic architectural constructions in oak, mahogany, rosewood, and walnut. Some were built into the recess of a room in the manner of a French *lit en alcove*; others imitated the *lit d'ange* or *lit à la duchesse*. With side curtains drawn back, they domed, winged, or hovered high above with phantasmagoric carvings, lavish swags, and garlands of gilded tassels.

By the end of the Victorian era, metal beds became the rage. Delicate, airy, white iron frames or brass beds with sturdy headboards and footboards, sporting new cotton mattresses—less likely to attract bacteria and bedbugs—ushered in a refreshing, ventilated feeling. It was the beginning of the kind of bedrooms we find so alluring today.

Deep in visual dimension and piling texture upon texture, this lavishly-colored baldachin-centered bedroom, doubly tented in yards of fabric, conjures up exotic scenarios in some maharajah's palace when Victoria was not only Queen of England but also Empress of India—a title she loved. Design: David Barrett; Photo: © image/dennis krukowski

A sweetly rendered pastel Victorian doll house, beribboned illustrations of nursery rhymes, a corner cabinet of bibelots, and a delicately scaled antique white iron crib lend magic to a charming wallpapered children's room. Interior design: Diane Soucy, Wall-to-Wall Interiors; Photo: Rob Karosis

Decked out with buttons and bows, tufted brocade and leather, a swaggering bed and an exaggerated mirror, this heavy-handed but authentic Victorian master bedroom in Aspen harkens back to the rich Colorado mining town's original gas-lit, ostentatious heyday. Design: Richard and Patricia Kent with Ron Kanan; Photo: Dave Marlow/Aspen

A richly textured interior environment that reads like the autobiography of a person or page from a Thomas Hardy novel comes to fascinating life through decorative elements with a Victorian feel, such as the apple-green bed, the lace-swagged window, the fabric-laden table, and roses everywhere. Design: Christine McCabe; Photo: Tony Giammarino

Enveloped by elaborate walls of powdery pink and green and covered with a creamy crocheted spread, an infinitely romantic bed of white wrought iron and brass, fashionable in the last years of the Victorian era, embraces the light through lacy windows and exquisite period lighting fixtures. Design: Simpson House; Photo: Tim Street-Porter

Exuding both cozy appeal and airy grace, this idyllic private sanctuary blends outdoors and indoors—a notion Victorians introduced—through the fresh use of paint and with just a handful of well-chosen flowery flourishes around a stack of books and a crisp white bed. Design: Cameron, Cameron & Taylor; Photo: Peter Peirce

Dainty mauvy sprays of flowers reinforce the sensuously molded wooden frame of an 1870s
American Victorian sofa and make patchwork magic on the early Arts and Crafts bed. This
romantic attic hideaway is equipped with an old-fashioned stove to warm the night and a gently
smocked cloud-blue shade to let the morning in. Photo: Tim Street-Porter

A Victorian secret garden is brought inside a gabled bedroom through an all-enfolding wall abloom with roses, hollyhocks, and imaginary hiding places. The patchwork quilt bunched into the antique bassinet makes a sweet nest for teddy bears. The pretty bed, the vintage dolls, and dappled hobby horse all contribute to the tea party in progress. Photo: Tim Street-Porter

All the romance, rococo riches, and influence of exotic worlds thought of as Victoriana is reflected around this spun-sugar dressing table. The peach-and-lemon hued Aubusson rug lends cohesion to the gilded mirrors, spindly jardinières, chairs of English papier-mâché and Persian pearl inlay. Design: Tonin MacCallum; Photo: © image/dennis krukowski

Everything's coming up roses and sunflowers, lollipop-colored ginghams and seersuckers in this blissfully light-splashed, airily angled, contemporary interpretation of the Victorian motto that myriad satisfactions and cheerful ideas can be plucked from a summer garden. Design: Shane Miller; Photo: Tony Giammarino

A pair of as-found old wicker pieces—a curvy armchair and a magazine rack used for holding petunias—add to the Victorian sleeping-porch feeling of this barely decorated sleep perch in a heavenly bay window overlooking the seaward slope of San Francisco's streets. Design: Denise Nelson; Photo: David Duncan Livingston

The precious original woodwork about the doors and the carved caryatids around the original tiled fireplace in this 1890s New York townhouse invite the use of sumptuous clouds of
dusty rose and cream silk fabrics. Their soft hues also cue the atmospheric wallpaper and
Oriental rug. Design: Marcy Balk; Photo: Peter Peirce

The serene beauty of the cobweb-and-floral filigree in
this lavender and green stained-glass insert above
the columned partition of a sleep area suggests the
color scheme of this delightful Victorian bedroom and
sheds ample light on why the era holds such emo-
tional appeal for us today. Design: Smith & Smith;
Photo: Tony Giammarino

Sponged white walls, a strikingly skeletal hundred-year-old Ohio chandelier and a lovely Persian rug help
bring out the basically clean architecture of this nineteenth-century room as well as the whimsical strength of
a classic American Victorian bedroom set of quartered oak and Carrara marble—once part of a bride's
trousseau. Design: TK; Photo: © image/dennis krukowski

Massive, heavily carved wood, mock columns, and marble favored by Victorians need not mean clutter. In this meticulously ordered and boldly architectural bedroom of stripes and paisleys a man can find luxurious nightly respite from an overwhelming contemporay pace. Design: Marcy Balk; Photo: Peter Peirce

Achieving a mildly medieval-looking bed, the owner of this room was unwilling to yield scant floor space to a real headboard. So he designed a buffalo-hide cushion hanging by leather straps from brass rosettes, delightfully reiterated by ribbon-hung ornithological prints. More echo of Victorian times: the string-crocheted bedcover and tapestry roll pillow. Design: Marshall Watson; Photo: Keith Scott Morton

An intimate elegance suffuses this bedroom filled with rare pieces and coveted treasures such as the japanned Chippendale bureau chest, the superb Regency chair, and a dreamy, garden-fresh, hand-painted four-poster with a ruffled Victorian-style half-tester. Design: David Scott; Photo: Peter Peirce

The very definition of Victorian delicacy rustles through this cozy enclosure of *toile de Jouy* dripping with antique lace. All we crave from the British country houses of that era fill the charms of this bedroom: the matching bedding and wallpaper, a curvy Victorian chair with needlepoint pillow, a portrait of Cavalier King Charles puppies on the wall. Design: Tonin MacCallum; Photo: © image/dennis krukowski

Sleep and dreaming draw spellbinding forms from the swirly fantasies of Victorian design. The gilded-cage aura of this extraordinary nineteenth-century brass bed casts its enchantment over such other bedroom favorites of the time as a bentwood baby rocker, a curlicued caned chair, and a beautifully carved fruitwood armoire. Photo: Tim Street-Porter

An avid San Francisco collector's bedroom over-
flows with the highly ornamental furnishings and
bibelots of the Victorian mainstream. Blending
quaint, lush, and even florid objects—such as former gas lamps and a fabulous original tobacco-
velvet Turkish rocker with ancestral photographs—the room is made whole by its dazzling
walls, rugs, and ceilings.

The room is dominated by an examplary Renaissance Revival bed made of walnut. Its extravagant
details, carved oval and elliptical panels, the high-
falutin half-tester overhead, festooned with silken
braids, was very much in favor during the middle
Victorian period. It allowed the sleeper to draw
the drapery so as to insulate head and shoulders
against the nighttime cold. Photo: David Duncan
Livingston

Broad design inspirations from Queen Victoria's imperial expansion meld in this stunning contemporary bedroom: paisleys from the Near East, the late-Victorian enchantment with everything Japanese, pillows stacked five deep, the crocheted soutache on the bed skirt, Chesterfield settees, and balloon shades. Design: Marcy Balk; Photo: Peter Peirce

The rich, dark-mahogany four-poster silhouetted against the sun-blinding whiteness of Britain's African colonial sleeping quarters is dramatized in this Ralph Lauren safari bedroom, accessorized with cool cotton curtains, jungle-beaten vintage luggage, and a sisal rug evocative of the savannas. Design: Ralph Lauren; Photo: Bill Rothschild

A faintly medieval overhead hanging evokes the Victorian fondness for the cozy beds of earlier epochs and also plays up the lovely proportions of the iron-and-brass bedstead. Dressed in pink-and-pretty linens, the bed is surrounded by nineteenth-century furnishings. Design: Betty Sherill, McMillen, Inc.; Photo: Phillip H. Ennis

The rosy glow emanating from a collection of pink glass on the dark wood Victorian wallstand and on the flouncy dressing table, as well as the fanciful negligée rack and the warm-hued rosepoint rug make this bedroom both elegant and feminine. Design: Betty Sherill, McMillen, Inc.; Photo: Phillip H. Ennis

Swaying in the gentle afternoon breeze coming through the lace-veiled, open French doors of this nineteenth-century guest room, an antique Mexican hammock adds seductive siesta languor to such heights of Victorian refinement as the sinuously crafted brass chandelier, splendid metal bed, and collection of Tiffany vases. Photo: Tim Street-Porter

A beguilingly curved canopy bed cloisters itself for delicious privacy with gauzy hand-made cottons and delicate examples of ancient lace. Tucked under rough-hewn exposed beams, it sets the undisturbed mood of this hundred-year-old room in **Monterey Adobe.** Design: Courtesy of *Historic Preservation* magazine; Photo: David Duncan Livingston

A pristine white modern bed taps into the Victorian heritage of its delightful prairie farmhouse setting. The simple beauty of wainscoting inspires the use of just a few period conceits: the Oriental octagon bamboo table, a balloon-back chair, and a profusion of roses. Photo: David Duncan Livingston

Towards the end of the Victorian age, the Arts and Crafts Movement made a strong mark on how bedrooms were furnished both in England and the United States. Here, the motto of banishing frills in favor of the purest standards of handcraftsmanship resound through the exceptional woodwork, the upliftingly placed stained-glass windows, and the Art Nouveau lamps. Design: Greene & Greene Architects; Photo: Tim Street-Porter

The great diversity of design in Victorian furniture—much of it variations on past themes—particularly manifests itself in pleasing chairs with tactile richness. Here, two such examples dominate a unique masculine retreat unafraid of rose-strewn valences, organdy curtains, and silk-fringed velvet shawls. Design: Genevieve Faure; Photo: © image/dennis krukowski

Though architecturally old-fashioned and anchored by the marvelous folly of a colossal Victorian bed of peaks and panels and whirligigs, the lighthearted hand-painted border near the ceiling and the freshness of the pastel rugs makes this a very livable modern-day bedroom. Photo: © image/dennis krukowski

Innocence and sophistication share the treat of this very special bedroom. Fresh gingham checks and a tree-of-life wallpaper create a unique nook for reading, dreaming, and sleeping among a gallery of beguilingly framed Victorian heroines. Design: Tonin MacCallum; Photo: © image/dennis krukowski

Details served up with contemporary flair outline the windows and moldings with bold bands of red, thereby energizing the bay window area into a pretty stage for a charming array of Victoriana: an asymmetric Oriental bamboo chair, a white cast-iron lamp, and a curvaceous hand-painted writing desk. Design: Tonin MacCallum; Photo: © image/dennis krukowski

Cool white creature comforts culled with fantasy and wit create a totally original personal dream space. British Colonial mosquito netting used by Victorian explorers, antique wicker lamps, and enough pale-sailed nautica to carry any sleeper off into vast frothing waters of the seven seas surround this sensational bed heaped with precious heirloom linens. Design: Christine McCabe; Photo: Tony Giammarino

Piece by Piece *Bedrooms*
details

Luckily, the infinite variety of beds fabricated in Victorian England and nineteenth-century North America —with their airy grace, sometimes theatrical thrust or what we now perceive as humorous personality—are in plentiful supply today. Bedding, too, in recent years, has become positively nostalgic. Pillows, sheets and coverlets re-embrace a profusion of embroidery, ruffled eyelets, delicate appliques, satiny ribbons and lace inserts reminiscent of heirloom linens. Put a small Victorian settee or ottoman at the foot of the bed to hold extra duvets or throws. Try an old pine washstand or an American Gothic wardrobe against pale, well-lighted modern walls for a unique decorative statement. Turn on the romance with pink rosebuds, bunched violets and cascading wisteria—all Victorian patterns once again in fashion for carpets, upholstery fabric and wallpaper.

Victorian Bamboo

Genuine Oriental Bamboo chairs and tables, as well as furniture turned to simulate bamboo in England and America, are among the loveliest decorative pieces remaining from Victorian times. Like this exquisite, signed, New York-made nineteenth-century chest of drawers with a tilted oval mirror, their scale and form suits today's bedroom styles. They gain luxurious freshness against fabric-covered walls and lavish window treatments.
Design: Cullma + Kravis; Photo; Michael Mundy

Young Victoriana

The perennial charm of antique children's furniture is reflected in some of the enchanting Victorian dollhouses, collections of Victorian dolls, pint-size bentwood rocking chairs and bentwood infant rockers to be found in atique shops and flea markets. They can serve as atmospheric accessories in today's bedroom, whether or not a child is present.

Victorian Exotica

Mosquito netting lends a ravishingly romantic and adventurous aura to a bedroom. These veiled contraptions hanging from the ceiling were first encountered by Queen Victoria's famous explorers in Africa, Asia, and the Middle East. They are now widely stocked in many retail outlets.

Papier-Mâché Chairs

Papier mâché chairs were a product of the highly experimental Victorian period and with their black emphatic forms stand wonderfully silhouette-like against the frilly and diaphanous feminine fabrics we favor for romantic bedrooms. Originated in the Far East, these curvaceous pieces made of hardened paper pulp, chalk, glue, sand were lacquered or japanned and were sometimes inlaid with mother-of-pearl and were introduces in England via France in the mid 1800s.

The Fine Crafts

Private passions unfold in this highly personalized sanctuary for rest and relaxation. The bed is smothered with roses and patchwork quilts. The Arts and Crafts nighttable is decked with cleverly framed photos and a prized opaque-glass, turn-of -the century lamp. Design: Linda Marder; Photo: Tim Street-Porter

The Romantic Bed

Nothing romances a bedroom more than a shining brass bed lavished with a gathering of creamy, silken pillows. Here, a truly satisfyng dreamtime soufflé of hand-stitched confections prove a valentine to the theory that you can never have too many ruffled and beribboned pillows on a a pretty bed.

Anthony Antine
Antine Associates, Inc. Interior Design
750 Park Avenue
New York, NY 10021

Anthony Catalfano Interiors Inc.
71 Newbury Street, Suite 3
Boston, MA 02116

Julie Atwood
216 Petaluma Boulevard
Petaluma, CA 94952

Marcy Balk
44 West 76th Street #1
New York, NY 10023

David Barrett
131 East 71st Street
New York, NY 10021

Roger Bartels, Architect
27 Elizabeth Street
South Norwalk, CT

Ben Theodore Inc.
70 Charles Street
Boston, MA

Kathy Best
258 29th Avenue
San Francisco, CA 94121

Cameron, Cameron & Taylor
  Design Associates
204 Columbia Heights
Brooklyn, NY 11201

Canac Kitchens
360 John Street
Thornhill, ON, Canada
L3T 3M9

Leighton Candler
1150 Fifth Avenue
New York, NY 10028

Dianne Chapman
3380 Washington Street
San Francisco, CA 94118

Robert Clark & Raymond LeCuyer
Mill Lane at Wickham
Mattituck, NY 11952

James Coursey
Coursey Design Consultants
The Manse
Heath, MA 01346

Tammy L. Couture
P. O. Box 2
West Barnstable, MA 02668

Cullman & Kravis, Inc.
Interior Decoration for Collectors
  of Fine Art and Antiques
790 Madison Avenue
New York, NY 11952

Karen Day
409 East Cooper Avenue #3
Aspen, CO 81611

Cheryl Driver
38 Stanford Shopping Center
Palo Alto, CA 94304

Ellen Lemer Korney
Ellen Lemer Korney Associates
10170 Culver Boulevard
Culver City, CA 90232

Mark Epstein
340 East 66th Street
New York, NY 10021

Faye Etter
Etter Interiors
8 Varnick Road
Newton, MA 02116

Jessica Flynn
5 West Falmouth Highway
Falmouth, MA 02540

Rena Fortgang
27 Forest Avenue
Locust Valley, NY 11560

Gary McBournie Inc.
33A North Main Street
Sherborn, MA 01770

Carol Ann Germana
P. O. Box 449
Calverton, NY 11933

Gail Greene
200 East 58th Street
New York, NY 10022

Mark Hampton
654 Madison Avenue
New York, NY 10021

Bobbi Henley
173 Walton Street
Englewood, NY 07631

Terry Pieciak
Interior Design Consultants
54 Nash Hill Road
Ludlow, MA 01056

Marilyn Katz
Interior Design, Ltd.
630 Park Avenue
New York, NY 10022

The Iron Shop
400 Reed Road
Broomall, PA 19008

Ron Kanan
Kanan Construction
P. O. Box 649
Aspen, CO 81611

Kitchen Aid
701 Main Street
St. Joseph, MI 49085

Knackstedt, Inc.
Mary K. Interiors
2901 North Front Street
Harrisburg, PA 17110

Martin Kuckly
Kuckly Associates, Inc.
506 East 74th Street
New York, NY 10021

Judith Levithan & Michael Orsini
155 East 55th Street
New York, NY 10022

Lipkin Warner Design & Planning
P. O. Box 2239
Basalt, CO 81621

Lisa Bonneville Design
68 Summer Street
Manchester, MA 01944

Lynn C. Avenoso Design Services
203 Bay Avenue
Patchogue, NY 11772

Manijeh M. Emery
M. M. Interiors
P. O. Box 160
Osterville, MA 02655

Tonin McCallun
21 East 90th Street
New York, NY 10022

Mark Wilkinson Furniture UK
Overton House, High Street
Bromham Chippenham
Wiltshire ENG SN15 3HA

Marshall Watson Interiors Ltd.
105 West 72nd Street, 9B
New York, NY 10023

Christine McCabe
200 East 16th Street
New York, NY 10003

McMillen, Inc.
Betty Sherrill
155 East 56th Street
New York, NY 10022

Miller Stein
1160 Chestnut Street
Menlo Park, CA 94025

Monte Berkoff Kitchens
295 Nassau Boulevard South
Garden City, NY 11530

Lee Napolitano
55 Woodland Drive
Oyster Bay Cove, NY 11771

Louis Navarrete
301 West 108 Street, #4F
New York, NY 10025

Barbara Ostrom
Crossroads Corporation Center
Mahwah, NJ 07430

Victoria Pasko
P. O. Box 51
Mannesquan, NY 08736

Dennis Pendalari
Pendalari Historic Interiors
27 Olde Homestead Drive
Marston Mills, MA 02648

Albert Pensis/KPS
200 Lexington Avenue
New York, NY 10016

Ralph Lauren Home
1185 Avenue of the Americas
New York, NY 10036

Lynn Robinson
34 Audrey Avenue
Oyster Bay, NY 11771
Jenny & Bob Salzmann
Scarlet's Antiques
166 Main Street
Northport, NY 11768

Candra Scott
30 Langton Street
San Francisco, CA 94103

David Scott
151 East 80th Street #1
New York, NY 10021

Gail Shields-Miller
Shields & Company Interiors
149 Madison Avenue, Suite 201
New York, NY 10016

Marjorie Shushan
15 West 53rd Street 35-A
New York, NY 10019

Summer Hill Ltd.
2682H Middlefield Road
Redwood City, CA 94063

Teri Seidman Interiors
150 East 61st Street
New York, NY 10021

Diane Soucy
Wall to Wall Interiors
23 Dearborn Street
Millford, NH 03055

Waverly
A Division of F. Schumacher & Co.
79 Madison Avenue
New York, NY 10016

Camille Belmonte, Mary Beth Galvin
Wellesley Design Center
868 Worcester Road
Wellesley, MA 02181

Carol O'Brien, Susan Harris
Wellesley Design Consultants
170 Linden Street, Suite 2B
Wellesley, MA 02482-7919

Cecilia K. Wheeler
25 Bay Avenue
Sea Cliff, NY 11579

Miriam Wohlberg
2325 Lindenmere Drive
Merrick, NY 11566

Wood-Mode Inc.
1 Second Street
Kreamer, PA 17833

Zoe Compton
Zoe Murphy Compton Ltd.
321 Sopris Creek Road
Basalt, CO 81621

Photographers

Billy Cunningham
140 Seventh Avenue Apt. 4C
New York, NY 10011

Phillip H. Ennis
114 Millertown Road
Bedford, NY 10506

Tony Giammarino
419 Williamsdale Drive
Richmond, VA 23235-4059

Mick Hales
Greenworld Pictures Inc.
North Richardsville Road, R.D.2
Carmel, NY 10512

Peter Jaquith
6 Pleasant Street
Beverly, MA 01915

Dennis Krukowski
329 East 92 Street
Suite 1D
New York, NY 10128

Rob Karosis
855 Islington Street
Portsmouth, NH 03801
David Duncan Livingston
1036 Erica Road
Mill Valley, CA 94941

Dave Marlow
The Marlow Group, Inc.
421 AABC Suite J
Aspen, CO 81611

Keith Scott Morton
39 West 29th Street
New York, NY 10001

Michael Mundy
25 Mercer Street
New York, NY 10013

Stewart O'Shields
16 East 82nd Street
New York, NY 10028
Peter Peirce
307 East 44th Street #1122
New York, NY 10017

Bill Rothschild
19 Judith Lane
Wesley Hills, NY 10952

Stanley Rumbough, Inc.
14 Andrews Road
Greenwich, CT 06830

William Stites
1075 75th Street Ocean
Marathon, FL 33050

Tim Street-Porter
2074 Watsonia Terrace
Los Angeles, CA 90068

Steve Vierra
P. O. Box 1827
Sandwich, MA 02593

Kathryn Livingston writes on art, architecture, and interior design for magazines, books and television. Her articles have appeared in *Harper's Bazaar, Gourmet, Connoisseur, Conde Nast Traveler, Travel & Leisure,* and *Town & Country.* During her fourteen years at *Town & Country* magazine, she reported on lifestyles across the U.S. and interviewed creative catalysts in Paris, Milan, London, Hamburg, Bangkok, Dakar, Rio de Janiero, Toronto, and Mexico City. She has traveled to remote Himalayan villages, Mauritanian Sahara outposts, and Guatemalan highlands where she encountered extraordinary handcrafts. She served as creative consultant for Time Warner's 130-segment CBS-TV series "Your Mind and Body" and is the author of a book on *Bed Linens,* part of Knopf's *Chic Simple* series. Ms. Livingston is the recipient of several awards, among them the Penney-Missouri Award for excellence in magazine journalism.